STORM DAMAGE

First published in 2025 by
The Dedalus Press
13 Moyclare Road
Baldoyle
Dublin D13 K1C2
Ireland

www.dedaluspress.com

ISBN 978-1-915629-47-0 (paperback)
ISBN 978-1-915629-46-3 (hardback)

Dedalus Press titles are available in Ireland
from Argosy Books (www.argosybooks.ie) and in the UK
from Inpress Books (www.inpressbooks.co.uk).

Cover artwork, 'Ginkgo Leaves in Red' by Nina Browne,
by kind permission. *www.ninabrowne.com.*

Dedalus Press receives financial assistance from
The Arts Council / An Chomhairle Ealaíon.

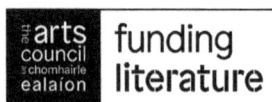

the arts council / chomhairle ealaion   funding literature

STORM DAMAGE

CATHERINE ANN CULLEN

DEDALUS PRESS

Contents

≈

Storm Damage / 9

Pencilling the Dates / 10

Lullaby on Your Eighteenth Birthday / 13

Chrysalis / 15

Fetishes / 16

First Tattoos / 18

Wintering / 20

My Bones Sing / 22

Hourglass / 23

Rope / 24

Subsidence / 25

Blown It / 26

Shell House Folly, Bushy Park / 27

his spine my abacus / 28

Love in the Tenters / 30

Ice House / 31

Wobbly Plates / 33

Love Poem at the Shrine of Saint Valentine / 34

Ghost Crabs at Strathmere / 35

Future Perfect / 36

Sajid Muzher / 37

Paper Boats / 38

Al-Mutanabbi Street / 40

Stone / 41

John O'Leary Roundel / 42

Maud Gonne Roundel / 42

FIVE PIECES ON THE NORTH INNER CITY FOLKLORE COLLECTION

Song: Who Goes There? / 43

Monto Cross / 44

Docker's Button Haiku / 45

Sadiron / 46

Song: Magdalene Laundry Blues / 47

Brigid of the Bargain Bins / 48
Shadow / 49
The Stitchin' / 50
Sanctuary / 51
Secret Birthday / 52
Ciotóg / 55
Plámás / 56
Song: Camac, Crooked Friend / 57
Flood / 59
Swift City / 61
She Wishes for Yeats's Last Muse / 62
Memory of My Rothar / 63
Song: Molly Alone / 64
The Measure of My Song / 66
Calliope's Song / 67
How to Learn / 69
Not Your Princess / 70
When the Bough Breaks / 72
A Broadside for Frank Harte / 74
Cabin Boy / 75
Triskele / 76
Hieronymus Bosch at the Great Fire
of 's-Hertogenbosch / 78
Reflection / 79
The Divil's Not Bad / 80
My Father in Mount Jerome / 81
Helmet Crab / 83
Listening to Moon River / 84

NOTES / 85
ACKNOWLEDGEMENTS / 88

in affectionate memory of my parents, Jack and Mary,
and of beloved friends Ak, Catherine, Colum,
Katie (Caroline), Linda, Orla and Síle –
i mo chroí go deo

Storm Damage

i.m. Mam

When I went to collect my bicycle
from the hospital where you'd withered,
the storm had recast it as an autumn sculpture.

The grooves between frame and tyres were choked.
Wheels vanished into flares of amber and yellow.
Here and there, a green frond interlaced the spokes.

It almost took my breath away

this blaze of light in the half-dark.
I took time to trundle my bike down the path,
loath to dislodge the gifted leaves too fast.

With each turn, they fell away, singly or in huddles:
behind me, a trail of fire,
before, the way home.

Pencilling the Dates

Every morning of the holiday,
our five-year-old collected the eggs,
clambered up to the wooden table,
pencilled the date on each brown shell,

till unexpectedly she handed me
a membrane where no shell had formed:
opal, opaque,
the shadow of life inside it.

When I touched its rubber skin
I had to turn my head
at the memory of those two small moons
that fell from their orbit.

The first I buried
at Mission Dolores,
wrapped in tissue with a note:
Here lies one who was loved and expected.

I could not take her home,
entrusted her to her dream helpers
among the Muwekma Ohlone,
the Gold Rush fevered and the earthquake dead.

We had not settled on a name
so I murmured Frances, Francesca,
tucked her in at the roots of an oak,
more familiar than the cypress trees.

I walked away as the sun watered,
and an old man
working the rose garden
rested on his spade and raised his hat.

The other birthed as I doubled over
in a London restaurant
and felt him pulse out,
a world of dead hopes:

John Henry, after our two fathers,
and the folk song
of the steel-driving man
blasting through rock.

I cried for my small catastrophes,
my inhospitable womb,
for the women who would have been glad
of their passing so early.

Our pencilled dates were erased.
There was no longer an August star
born in a shower of the Perseids,
no longer a softness in sharp November.

To the young doctor who claimed they were nothing
I wanted to say, *you too were nothing once,*
but perhaps your mother dreamed of you,
had faith that you would come.

I had put all this away
but it rushed back with the touch
of the rubber egg
in our daughter's hand.

And when I told her gently
about the lost ones,
she pencilled their portraits
in jeans and checked shirts:

Francesca with her hair tied up,
John Henry with his long fringe,
smiling out of their teenage bedrooms
as if nothing had happened.

Lullaby on Your Eighteenth Birthday

for Stella

Push, rush, midnight hush

You came babbling out of my body
in the witching hour.
The midwife said
this one was here before.

And I felt blessed to call you child,
to call you daughter,
to baptise you with milk
if not with water.

Hush now baby, Mamma's gonna love you

Night-feeding, crooning
under the covers,
I felt the long reach back
through mothers of mothers:

your father's kin, bundling their broods
out of hostile ground:
refugees in Spain and Sicily,
lulling in tongues lost and found

On wings of the wind o'er the dark rolling deep

and mine with their Irish lenitions,
their curling Norman tongues,
all of them soothing their flocks
with bird-song, wind-songs, sea songs:

Coroo, dawhah, arrorró,
ninna, nanna, fais dodo,
lullay, lullaye, seoithín seo-hó

Your blood, the blood of all
who brought us to this place,
your mouth small on my breast,
your eyes huge on my face.

I made you a morning song –
remember this?
We start the day
with a smile and a kiss …

You drank the shapes of words,
till you weaned yourself away.

Stay out all night, my darling,
sleep like a child all day.

Caithfimid suas is suas,
Caithfimid suas an páiste,
Caithfimid suas í suas is suas í,
'S tiocfaidh sí 'nuas amárach.

We'll throw her up, up,
We'll throw her up so high,
We'll throw her up, up,
until she'll reach the sky.

Chrysalis

The robin sings a fence around the garden.
Note upon note, he builds his party wall.
Imperious, impervious to doubt,
he corners the market and sets out a stall

that brooks no browsers. Deep in the firethorn hedge,
he monitors the boundaries unseen.
There's no go to his pulsing traffic signal,
his stop sign never changes, flashes green,

until a mate is drawn by his performance.
He sings her in. The rest, at a safe distance,
storm his electric fence with their own tunes,
test its vibrations with a loud resistance.

Fenced in the yard, cocooning with the birds,
I wind myself a chrysalis of words.

Fetishes

A whisper of silver
slips into my palm
from the silk pouch
Justine proffers.

Slowly his great wings come into focus,
his raised sword,
his foot on the head of his old friend.

I notice the family of worry dolls
ranged in order of size
on the wobbly table
by Stella's bed.

Moira crochets a blanket
in healing colours:
greens, blues, violet.

Laura brings me a felted sugar skull
with embroidered flowers for eyes
and three stitched teeth bared
above a gold tassel.

Our daughters manifest
a breast of hammered tin
from Santa Luciella in Naples.

I finger its ridged frame,
wrap it in the blanket for the hospital,
tuck it into my coat pocket
for every appointment.

There are so many appointments.

Every so often
a glim fairy
leaves a fresh candle
by the front door.

A Traveller woman named Josie
who stops to take some of the clutter
laid out in front of my parents' house

takes hold of my hand,
then rummages in her car
for a flask of holy water
in the shape of Our Lady.

I place it with the phial of shaman water,
soothing citrus, rose and lavender,
that Justine brought last time.

Today she is awkward.
I wasn't sure you'd want this:
a miraculous medal
of Michael the Archangel.

I hug her,
tell her that these days
I embrace all the ways of loving,

grasp whatever anyone
holds against the dark.

First Tattoos

I never had the urge
to be marked or pierced,
left it to friends
to embrace the belly-button jewel
for a roundy birthday,
the discreet gecko
inked on a shoulder blade,

until the glamorously named Design Scan
to plan my radiotherapy.
The therapist's name was Amber,
that was glamorous too,
but not the sheet of rough paper
she offered as a modesty blanket
while I removed my clothes above the waist.

Did anyone tell you
you'd be getting some tattoos today?
Three small dots:
one in the centre,
one on each side,
to help us line you up
for the machine.

Like bullseyes, I think,
as I feel them scratch onto my skin,
something to find in a rifle sight;
pinholes through which to view
the eclipse.

Afterwards I look for them in the mirror.
At the base of my breastbone,
a cobalt dot
pinpoints the centre
of foreboding.

The others evade me at first,
till I find them camouflaged
by a scatter of freckles:
two satellites pulsing
through an indifference of stars.

Wintering

Barely September and I feel winter's bite,
look skyward for my brent
to come early.

'Burnt' geese, from the Norse,
for your charcoal feathers
smouldering over frozen waters
to smoke on our damp fields,
our winter a balm
against icy tundra.

Your feathers remember the sky,
flights mapped in the compass
of your bones,
once so low over my head
I could hear your wings
thump, thump the air.

I'll be counting on you,
your straggling lines an abacus,
clocking up another winter.

Though I listen,
just one in a hundred lets go
a lonesome cry
as you straddle the dawn again,
make for some hollow
to sit out of the wind,

faithful like me
to this city park
for your twentieth year.

How was it for you,
the breeding season,
escaping the white fox?

My Bones Sing

i.m. Breda Wall Ryan

The weather has turned cold,
but I cradle my mug on the threshold,
hands warm, bare feet numb on the paving.

A robin flings himself at a rival in the window.
A blackbird gorges furtively on ivy berries.
The *Scarlet River* lily blooms like fire.

Our one tree is an extravagance of apples.
Every morning, I pluck windfalls from wet grass,
every evening, peel, core, excise bruises.

I stew until the house is dizzy with sweetness.

Neighbours have all been gifted.
I have run out of containers.
Still, they fall.

When the screen found three stones
in the seedless fruits of my breasts,
you sent me your number.

I keep your poems by me
to remind me to hear
my bones singing.

I send you warmth from my cupped hands,
the fragrance of a glut of apples,
two birds and a river of fire.

Hourglass

i.m. Orla Parkinson

When I heard that I'd seen you
for the last time
in the library
with the pain
in your eyes,
I remembered how
the hourglass you admired,
delicate in its brass frame,
toppled from the mantelpiece.

I wanted to turn it over
once more
and watch the salt
run through its slender waist.

The fragments
I gathered
were light as air,
so fine
it was a wonder
they had ever
measured time.

And though I swept and swept
where the salt had scattered
on the hearth,
for months afterwards,
among the ashes,
I kept finding
white grains
and needles of glass.

Rope

That frayed loop between the trees
on our stretch of stream
is altered.

I no longer see
the swing where
we took turns to span
the trickle of the Poddle,
lazily tipping
one side,
then the other,
faces dreamy
in the dappled light.

Although you were far away
when they found you,
each morning
at the corner of my eye
that blue rope shocks.

Subsidence

I did not know the weight of a heart
could sink a house. But where the front door
stood, only the lintel shows above ground now.

Today I squeezed onto the landing floor,
climbed down to where you slump in the cellar.

But we had no cellar. Here at the countertops
we drank the sun for years, with coloured straws
bent to savour the last drops.

Soon I'll take the children to the attic
to breathe some light. There the sun will set
in the window and the houses opposite
reflect the morning.
                    When the rays get
to your heart, my love, they're bound to shift it.

I'd carry you up myself if I could lift it.

Blown It

They may not want us back,
the fox loping up Grafton Street,
or the vixen pausing to look
into the phone
of an essential worker
on the Ha'penny Bridge.

I imagine them breezing by
the deserted perfume counter
at Brown Thomas,
wrinkling their snouts
at our fey concoctions
and spraying real musk
on the extravagant bottles.

Shell House Folly, Bushy Park

Every Sunday
she holds us to her ear,
inhales our brittle music
between the snap of fir-tree mulch
and the heron's high scream.

What persists are her sturdy walls,
the deliberate, stone-on-stone
concoction of romance,
and here and there, a crust of cockle shells
bonded with plaster.

Graffiti glows over fag-ends of a sesh:
broken bottles, cans, a plastic bag.

Every Sunday we remember
our old lives: parties, teenage wilding,
and the waitress in Bewleys
who told us, 'I don't mind if you lie,
as long as you lie beautifully.'

Through the window sockets,
the green eyes of the stagnant lake gleam.

his spine my abacus

Let others
praise their lovers'
faces, eyes:

I celebrate
how his carriage
articulates,

his circuit
for mind-to-bone
messages,

the carillon
that orchestrates
his movement.

Nakedness
needs no other
adornment:

worry beads,
a rosary of stones,
one chord.

Algebra *noun*:
the reunion of
broken parts:

not broken,
we are islands
with bridges.

Thirty-three
seeds my fingers
harvest,

product
of two primes.
Each night

I learn to
count – my abacus
his spine.

Love in the Tenters

Over the Tenters, clouds are flocks of sheep
whose wool escapes in wisps, drifts down the air.
Were I a weaver, love, I'd bag the stuff,
and spin a coat of sky for you to wear.

This is where my mouth and yours first met,
winding our slow thread home beyond the Coombe,
our footsteps crossing over Weavers Square,
where, by their ghostly looms, ghost weavers loom.

Here, like poor weavers in a winter storm,
we'll tenter our cloths before the alehouse fire.
What you don't stretch might shrink, so hook your dreams
and pull them tight and wide as your desire.

We've searched the eyes of ghosts and not-yet-ghosts,
learned to weave poplin lives like all our ilk:
across the warp of wool or worsted yarn,
look for the weft of silk.

Ice House

After a night of snow,
sleet drifted obliquely
across the Boston morning.

A snowplough churned by
and the street was a river
frilled with white lace.

We crunched a salt path
towards the ring of voices,
smack of gloves on snow,

till we reached the corner
where it rose unsteadily,
glassy block on block.

A man stretched
to plaster a film of snow
over the top,

while three children
patted fistfuls of powder,
their mittens sticking to the sides.

One girl stopped,
hand mid-air,
cheeks hectic red.

She shouted,
come and see!
ran to the curved entrance.

Her father smiled.
We stooped low,
stood up to magic:

just you and I
inside a snowglobe
not yet shaken.

Wobbly Plates

On the morning of our wedding,
I gift you two wobbly plates,
pale blue, bright green,
tied loosely with twine.

Let us begin
shy of the surface,
sweet as broken biscuits
sold cheaply in old shops.

Since our beloved earth
bulges out of its sphere,
and sky has no shape
of its own,

what harm if you and I
buckle together,
green, blue,
askew?

On the morning of our wedding
I gift you two wobbly plates,
the bulging earth,
the shapeless sky.

Love Poem at the Shrine of Saint Valentine

Meet me by the accidental icon of love,
clubbed to death as birds mated
on Roman rooftops.

Before he lost his head,
they say he restored the eyes and ears
of his jailer's daughter.

Still she would not smash her idols
as she watched him trail towards death,
heard the crowd's enjoyment.

Some say his heart is here,
in the casket tied
with silk ribbon.

His skull is crowned with flowers in Rome,
his bones scattered across a dozen cities.
He was not martyred for love,

but on Saint Valentine's day,
let's take what romance we can
from the contrivance:

lose our heads
to a backdrop of birdsong,
be restored to our senses.

Ghost Crabs at Strathmere

The beach was alive with ghost crabs
burrowing into the soft sand,
our giddy teenager and her friend
running after them like children.

You threw your straw hat over one
on the hard sand at the water's edge,
unveiled it as the girls looked on.

The crab stood like a matador,
holding its business claw aloft,
eyes on stalks like a cartoon character,

until he found his moment,
slowly waltzed towards a sandhole,
all the time facing our mesmerised quartet.

Too late I grabbed my phone,
preserved only a swirl of sand,
and two young women
sidestepping out of the frame.

Future Perfect

No conscription letters will have landed
and the young men will be at home
in their own countries.

The therapists will have exhausted collective trauma,
moved on to divorce and phobias.

Pedestrians will have tut-tutted at the van
parked askew outside the station
and ignored the sound
of a car backfiring in the next street.

No one will have spoken in code,
testing for shibboleths,
and the children
playing football on the beach
will have dribbled their ball home.

Sajid Muzher

As you lay dying, you raised a victory sign,
Sajid of the gentle hands.

Those who shot you must have missed
your volunteer uniform and orange jacket.

But you were more vivid than any jacket,
seventeen summers brighter than the roses
wreathing your funeral photograph.

Life-sized.

Paper Boats

I fold my poems into boats
to hazard your shore,
an origami flotilla
bobbing towards the occupation.

Between the creases
some words are legible:
'resistance' on the sail,
'defiance' on the flag.

And when the gunships
spot the word 'freedom'
rushing the coast,
their shells will rupture my fleet.

The boats will sink and then rise,
or erupt skywards and then fall,
scattering rags of verse
across the water.

But I've folded some so carefully
that their blind sides
might float
past security.

Perhaps one will beach
where children have played
and you will spread it
like a map in your hands

and know that someone
whose rage is not brave
will fold poems into boats
to open on your sands

till on every shore
are hands folding boats
and your waters are white
with fleets of our hopes.

Al-Mutanabbi Street

This street named for a poet
runs with booksellers and cafés,
a river where poems float
remembering the lost.

When they bombed
the bazaar of manuscripts,
the words copied by hand
caught fire.

The cinders rose into the air
and landed on pages, on heads,
and the poets found themselves
in a new fever of writing.

Stone

for my great-granduncles, Matthew and Michael Moroney of Tralee

Your brother set your sentence on his stone.
Your name leapt from the note. He held his breath,
surveyed the lines, then laid them in reverse,
all from the upper case: SENTENCED TO DEATH.

The largest font was wood. His fingers shook
but he composed the poster just the same,
took the packed form down to the proofing press.
His friend hand-rolled the ink over your name.

He smuggled home the uncorrected proof,
sign of the closeness of a brother's touch,
the intimacy of compositor with letters,
forming with care the words that weighed too much,

not knowing, as he set SENTENCED TO DEATH
what space was left before your final breath.

John O'Leary Roundel

Romantic Ireland's still alive and twitching,
though, fingers crossed, she's made her bloody will.
O'Leary husbands, without self-enriching,
Romantic Ireland's till.

Joyce's 'Last Fenian', who'd have had his will
if not for all the spying and the snitching,
the man of property who paid the bill,

the editor whose pen was always itching
to point out to the poets their lack of skill.
While Yeats (through rosy eyes) finds her bewitching,
Romantic Ireland's still.

Maud Gonne Roundel

I'll work my magic lantern's slide projection
and meet the thrust of empire with the tragic
scenes of eviction, famine and abjection.
I'll work my magic.

The flutter of Union Jacks turns me dysphagic.
I'll hoist my bloomers for the royal inspection:
like flags, their value's merely camouflagic.

We'll soar above the Famine Queen's objection,
and if this time our wings are burned, I'll cadge
Icarus a chance at rising, resurrection:
I'll work my magic.

Song: Who Goes There?

for Molly O'Reilly (1900–1950)

I was sent to learn dancing at Liberty Hall,
But Jim Connolly's talks sent me reeling,
For my home stamping ground of the tenement sprawl
Needed more than mere toeing and heeling.
Now they ask, *who's the brat who's so light on her feet,*
Who's dancing rings round us whenever we meet?
I'm Molly O'Reilly from Gardiner Street,
If anyone asks, *who goes there?*

Jim gave me the gift of a messenger pouch
On a brown leather belt with a buckle,
For he saw at the sidestep that I was no slouch
And to union nor crown I'd not truckle.
With the belt on my hip I could run hell for leather,
God knows our poor army was cobbled together,
But I gave the Peelers a bit of old blether
If ever they asked, *who goes there?*

A soup kitchen queen by the age of thirteen,
A firebrand with rifles to smuggle,
Unfurling the flag, the uncrowned harp on green,
On the eve of the Easter Week struggle.
Then from pillar to post as the shells smoked the air,
I ran rebel notes on a wing and a prayer,
I'm Molly O'Reilly, the devil may care,
If anyone asks, *who goes there?*

I'm Molly O'Reilly, the Summerhill hare,
If anyone asks, *who goes there?*

Monto Cross

for Margaret Carroll (c1875-1917), a prostitute in the Monto

As she lay dying in the joiner's tenement,
the priest disdained to bless her,
for Margaret Carroll had fleeced the man
her sister whacked with a poker
when he wouldn't cough up.

You could makeshift a cross
from twigs and string
but the joiner trawled the dockyard
for two scantlings of wood,
chiselled from each a rebate
so they sat snug together.

He lacquered his work with thin paint
till it was quite respectable.

When he got home,
the daughter who had been taken from her
was at her side.

Margaret had no strength left
but the cross was light as air,
lighter than any air in the choke of the Gloucester Diamond.

She clutched it with the hands
she had held up for her prison photograph.

It was black as a brothel poker,
black as she was painted,
black as the chemise a judge had once given
his favourite girl.

Docker's Button Haiku

The docks hiring fair:
faces like scrunched newspapers
waiting for the Read.

Foremen, deadpanning,
study lines of workers scribbled
beneath the scaffold.

Your father's button
storying your frayed lapel:
Deep Sea Coal Docker.

Sadiron

*Mid-18th century from 'sad', in the obsolete sense 'weighty',
and 'iron' (OED)*

Silent here
but for the thud, thud
of the tailor's goose.

No golden eggs
hide in its
heavy body.

The women fallen
between the cracks
smooth over and over:

crank the handle,
feed the mangle,
put through the wringer,

bear down
with the sadiron,
no great leveller:

the swollen hands
sanding its metal
no lady's hands,

their fingers
grasp the hot neck
gingerly,

eyes pricking,
skin coarsening,
they steam the linen.

Song: Magdalene Laundry Blues

I went down to the Magdalene laundry
looking for my sister there,
but I did not recognise her
for they'd shaved her long brown hair.

Can you hear my sister crying
in the early morning cold?
For they took her from her darling,
only one she had to hold.

She will wash your dirty linen,
she will scrub it hard and cheap
for the priest's house and the big house
so the filthy rich can sleep.

Can you hear your sister crying
just to hear you say her name?
Now they call her by a number
and they tell her she's to blame.

When she dreams, she dreams of prison.
When she dreams, she dreams of hell.
Only time she dreamed of heaven
was the night the angels fell.

Can you hear your sister crying
as she washes night and day?
But the stain of being a woman
she can never wash away.

Brigid of the Bargain Bins

Brigid lifts her toddler into the trolley
and tries to keep the twins busy
with a game of finding
the lowest numbers on the shelves.

She checks the prices of sliced pans,
weighs up own labels against known brands.
She knows they cut corners with prices,
sees through their tricks, has a few of her own.

She's Mary of the gale-force winds
that whistled through the flat
until she stretched clingfilm
inside the window frames.

She wears an oversized coat
that doubles as a blanket.

She will stretch her children's allowance
to cover the table,
take the bare look from the fridge,
fill up the lunchboxes.

She's skimped herself to dress the kids.
Under her coat, her threadbare hoodie
is ragged enough to hang on a tree
by a holy well.

At the checkout
she sees the first daffs,
wonders, now she's lost the weight,
if that blue dress might fit again.

Shadow

I keep it barred, that door into the dark,
although a weight still pushes at the bolt.
Most days I manage, only now and then
my grip grows slack, the lock gives with a jolt.
All in my mind.
                    But still he blocks the light,
across the threshold throws a livid shade,
his words, hot fists, still sounding in my head,
the thumping tune, a pounding serenade.

He never laid a hand on anyone.
The blows were subtle, finely honed, finessed,
and found their target. That was the only way
he knew to care, to crush what he loved best.

I hold myself, still, out of his shadow's sway,
grow towards light now, keep the dark at bay.

The Stitchin'

i.m. my grandmother, Kitty Cullen

You were buttonholed early for a factory girl,
the pattern of your life laid out
before you'd clocked up a dozen years.

The school bell called to others
but you tuned your ear to the mill's whistle,
threaded your way from the Cord Road

through the long eye of the railway arch.
You dreamed of taking the train
but your journey was a small track of stitches.

Whatever song was in your head,
your foot kept the rhythm of the treadle,
your head bent to the breakneck metronome

of door-knockers no-one answered.
At nineteen you left the stitchin'
for a production line of babies.

No wonder your clatter of children never rattled you,
after the mill's racket.
You never mentioned it, took no credit for your skill,

and when we hesitated over homework, you shook your head.
I only met the scholars coming home.
I only got to first book, you said.

Sanctuary

There is a place
where you're safe
from the chase,

where you know
whoever is 'It'
cannot go,

where you hear
the feet batter past,
your heart slams slow, slow,

where you've skipped out on death,
can stop running,
catch your breath.

The locked door feels good.
Uncross your fingers.
You're touching wood.

It feels like a game again.
You've reached
home, base, den.

Secret Birthday

Every year it looms out of the calendar,
the day your waters broke
and the midwife with the hard mouth
took your daughter.

Your husband
would not know what to say
if you told him.

Instead you listen for the knock,
search faces for one
who would be that age, this age,
with the lank fair hair
of your brother's friend.

Every year you feel
the pale silk of her head,
her length of limb,
the accusation of birthdays.

Your other children
evolve through time,
blue eyes smoking to green or grey,
white hair muddying to brown,
but in your mind she is suspended,
her face baby soft,
her birth colouring intact.

Every year remembers
you sitting in the doctor's
in your ankle socks and summer dress,
remembers everything organised
for her to vanish.

Song: Asking for a Friend

She was fourteen when it happened,
only know it happened hard:
hiding under baggy jumpers,
hearing whispers in the yard.
It's too late to change her story,
might have had a different end.
Would you refuse
her right to choose?
I'm asking for a friend.

I'm asking for the girl next door,
I'm asking for a friend.

They were thrilled to be expecting.
Soon she knew all hope was gone,
but the doctors couldn't save her
while the foetal heart beat on.
It's too late to change her fate
so change the law they would not bend.
Would you refuse
her right to choose?
I'm asking for a friend.

I'm asking for the girl next door,
the family on the second floor,
I'm asking for a friend.

She was a mother, sick with cancer.
Her consultant's view was clear:
termination was the answer –
pack your bags, can't happen here.

There's no way to change her story,
might have had a different end.
Would you refuse
her right to choose?
I'm asking for a friend.

I'm asking for the girl next door,
the family on the second floor,
the woman who can't take no more:
I'm asking for a friend.

Oh, Savita, Sheila, Anne,
X and Y, Michelle, Joanne,
and all the ones we'll never name,
who lived or died in fear and shame,
oh what woman, oh what man
would say you can't and not you can,
would make you face that lonely end?
I'm asking for a friend.

Women silenced, hear their voice,
had no chance, and had no choice,
would you refuse their right to choose?
I'm asking for a friend.

I'm asking for the girl next door,
the family on the second floor,
the woman who can't take no more,
the 'Magdalene' who scrubbed the floor,
I'm asking for a friend.

Ciotóg

This Irish word for a left-handed person also means awkward.

You form your letters with the devil's hoof,
that guilty hand we tie behind your back
to force you dextrous. An awkward customer,
we'll serve rightly, weird as widdershins, cack-

handed, writing with your arse-wiper, maladroit,
in touch with a free spirit we must cage.
We will beat out your demon, your gauche desire
to dance your spiders wild across the page.

Our right hands don't know
what your left is doing: wrist in a hook,
that sinister action hiding the words
as you write them, blotting your book.

In Irish you lean and squint, you've gone full rogue,
inclined to be wrong, clé, claon, ciotóg.

Plámás

This Irish word for flattery is said to derive from the French 'blancmange'.

Written down,
I would have been a shibboleth for your rough mouth
but your ear was untroubled
by my silent consonants.

You, who took my chambre for your seomra,
heard my blancmange as plámás.

I was opaque.
I insinuated my way onto your plate,
all air and aspiration.

The English with their chill shadow
called me 'cold shape',
served me with tarts and fools,
the Welsh made me a flummery of oatmeal.

But you bent your Irish ear to my blandishments,
your nose to neroli and rosewater.
You listened to my palaver,
used carrageen for my gelatine,
made me balm to bitter humours.

Flattery is a ham-fisted wheedler
but I am plámás:
I mesmerise you around my little finger,
soften my voice with almond milk,
smile up at you with pomegranate seeds,
coax you onto my junket,
slide deliciously down.

Song: Camac, Crooked Friend

The River Camac owes its name to the Irish word 'cam', or 'crooked'.

From Mount Seskin swift you spill,
Down the years and down the hill,
Turned the wheels from mill to mill,
In your heart they're turning still.
Cannons roar at Waterloo
Turned the summer morning dark,
Boney's troops were felled by powder
From your mills at Corkagh Park.

Chorus: Wind on, Camac, crooked water,
Swerve, Cam Uisce, like your name.
Dodge and bend,
Our crooked friend,
We'll love you just the same.

Orphan girl at Goldenbridge
Shared her sorrows as you passed,
Prisoner in Kilmainham Gaol
Heard you murmur at the last.
River run and Camac caper,
On your memories we depend:
Fairview Oil, Clondalkin Paper
Sing your stories to the end.

Chorus: Wind on, Camac, crooked water …

Destination Heuston Station,
One more traveller passing through,
Beneath the tracks, a lovers' tryst,
Fair Anna Liffey waits for you.
Through the city side by side,
Meet the Poddle on the way,
Crooked Camac, take our troubles,
Drown them all in Dublin Bay.

Chorus: Wind on, Camac, crooked water …

Flood

And the serpent poured water like a river out of his mouth after the woman, so that he might cause her to be swept away with the flood. But the earth helped the woman, the earth opened its mouth and drank up the river which the dragon poured out of his mouth. (Revelation 12:15–17)

While the barman joked, *have ye no homes to go to?*
she went down to the Royal Canal
and swaddled herself in a damp blanket
under Binn's Bridge.

Through the fabric
she felt the prick of the staple,
found the pinned note,
mouthed the words in the fractured light.

You unlawfully entered onto these lands and set up an encampment.
You are trespassing on the banks of the Canal which is a public
    amenity.
We call on you to vacate with your tents and belongings.
Unless you comply, we will ask the Gardaí to take action.

By the Royal Canal
without sovereignty
she sank down and wept,
where she had pitched her tents and made her songs,
for she had no home to go to.

And they flooded the walkway under Binn's Bridge
so she might float out of sight
on the holed boat of her dreams.

Earth, are you there
to open your mouth
and drink the flood?

Swift City

I am Gulliver sprawled on the shore.
You think you can tie me down
but I shake off the pins of your definitions.

I travel well.
I float rafts of words into the world
and they return solid as ships.

Ghosts materialise everywhere:
beneath their quaint speeches
are stories not yet finished.

I take nothing at face value:
I read the brass plates but weigh them
against words spray-painted on walls.

Sometimes I shrink before the others:
I am a mouse eye-balling a giant cat;
I am snagged in an eagle's talons and dropped in the sea.

My instincts are sharp.
I may be scarred and ragged, but
I drag myself home.

I am all about perspective:
The city is a speck lodged in my eye:
I will keep worrying it until I write it out.

She Wishes for Yeats's Last Muse

Trample my dreams until you stamp them out;
Reduce the sky's embroidery to flitters;
Where there is faith, enfeeble it with doubt
Till every strut and buttress has the jitters.

If you see me stilt-walk down the street
Or scale a ladder to my dreamy bed
Lest the foul earth contaminate my feet,
Lest I should meet the darkness head to head,
Tackle me to the unrelenting dirt
Till every word is shaped from graze and hurt.

Make me forgo the draught I use to dose up,
Keep all my demons ready for their close up,
Banish me from the circus and its thrall:
Give me his last muse or no muse at all.

Memory of My Rothar

after Patrick Kavanagh

Every old bike I see
Reminds me of my rothar,
Saddle breasting a garden hedge
Or nuzzling the gutter.

That wreck in Gardiner Street
Half-sprawling in the sun,
Its broken backlight stared at me:
It might have been the one.

And then again, those wheels
Flat to the path in Kimmage,
Rims listing, sad with rust:
They too unlocked your image.

Every old bike I see,
Familiar as a lover,
Leans towards me to say,
I am your stolen rothar.

Song: Molly Alone

I'm Ulysses' missus, the Odyssey girl,
Penelope giving her suitors a whirl,
a sloven, a slyboots, a sigh and a yawn,
not quite Molly Flanders, but no longer Bawn,
a mollification for any old savage
who couldn't distinguish a poem from a cabbage,
with three little letters I'm bound to express
Y-E-S, I said yes I will Yes.

I'm a straight white male construct, a Marian hymn
who sprang fully formed from the bedhead of Jim,
conceived with immaculate presence of mind
with malice aforethought and more thought behind.
Though his Nora's name starts with a definite no,
such a negative notion would hinder his flow,
for the Joycean female she must acquiesce
saying yes I said yes I will Yes.

If I could remember the half what he told me
I'd publish a book called *The Sayings of Poldy,*
but harum and scarum I drift on my bed,
telling all the cracked things that come into my head.
On page after page he must bring up my rear
till his hammering heart on my bosom I hear.
It's his own bloomin' fault I'm an adulteress
With his yes I said yes I will Yes.

For a world run by women I'd make a great case,
but my suffragette leanings are put in their place:
my creator would keep me in bed and indoors
and he asks that I cut him a piece of me drawers.

In Dublin's fair city, where the girls are so pretty,
you won't set your eyes on sweet Molly alone –
my brilliant perceptions will never be known,
just my breasts all perfume popping out of my dress
and my yes I said yes I will Yes.

The Measure of My Song

In Oxfam, an asylum seeker
with a stack of albums
and a gnarl of embroidery thread
told the cashier, *my name is Ovid.*

When I thread my pen,
a ribbon of song flows out,
stitching all the stories together
from creation to Caesar rocking YouTube.

I'm managing Apollo in the finals of the X Factor;
remixing Virgil on a makeshift desk;
bringing out a box-set called Shapeshifters;
writing a book in Irish.

The way the wind
mouths the reeds on the canal into music
reminds me of home.

My friends here tell me
I loved that place so much
I should never have been exiled.

If I went back they'd have my head.
It would float down the river singing.

Even then I'd moan
around my enemy's house
until he died and the earth spat up his body.

Even then you won't have heard
the measure of my song.

Calliope's Song

If my song is broken,
it is because I sing of rupture.

I sing the abduction
of the child picking flowers,
her tears for the scattered violets,
her screams for her mother.

I sing the mother calling,
the mother vanished into her loss.
I sing the mother who finds her child.
I sing the mother who will never find her child.

I sing the woman
who changes to repel
the violence
before the violence changes.

I sing the woman as pool of tears,
the woman forced to change,
the woman who transforms herself.

I sing of her who risks herself
to protect another.
I sing of her who bears witness.

I voice the woman who will never speak,
the silent call to the crisis line.
I sing of her who speaks and is not heard.
I sing of her who is heard.

I sing as a woman together with women
for the woman alone.
I sing for the survivors,
for those who are gone.

I sing because it is by singing
we tell stories
that must be told.

I sing for those who will never sing again.
I sing for those who may not sing.
I sing for those who believe they will not sing.

I sing for those who may sing again in time.
I sing with those whose song is not broken.
I sing for those who will sing again
even if their song
is broken.

How to Learn

for Doris Lessing

In the margins of a book on Sufism,
you scribbled notes and cartoon heads by turn,
the widest smile and jauntiest hat reserved
for one line: *start by mastering how to learn.*

You brooked no master, sought to grasp a name
that made no reference to any other,
to learn a definition of yourself
that did not style you daughter, wife or mother;

to learn to craft your failures into power,
for fiction makes a better job of truth,
to toss regrets and oughts and should-have-dones
into the whirlpools of old age or youth;

to learn that love's more arrow than embrace,
freedom, a door slammed, even in your face.

Not Your Princess

I might sleep again if only it would rain,
blue sky yielding like a dam wall
and a sea dark as your hair
breaking in waves against the windows.

I might sleep
if rain was the backing track
easing the segue from fretful dogs
to shutters rattling down, brushing
a patina of hush over the whole shebang.

Instead I shift and toss in a mirage
of coming to your door,
the water running in at the toe
and out at the heel
of my silk slippers.

My heart keeps knocking
until you hear it over the thunder.
You find me with a river
streaming down my hair and clothes.

You make up a bed for me
with seven mattresses.
The rain pitches itself
at the dark,

my wet mouth
finds your source.
We pitch together,
roll apart, and at last

I sleep soundly on your pea,
your myrtle leaf,
your bed of roses with one petal folded,
your single dark hair under the last mattress.

When the Bough Breaks

for Roger Bennett

When the bough breaks,
it waits for the woodturner
to press his ear to the bark
and hear the bowls singing.

> he brings home a block
> puts it on a pedestal
> worships it sideways

His lathe is a turntable,
his gouge a needle
playing the grooves of the wood,
never the same tune twice.

> the bowl's a haiku
> as if it were always there
> not a breath wasted

He is a poet of the sycamore.
He hears the secrets
whispered to the wood under distant stars
and binds them to its heart
with silver wire.

> in a certain light
> the milky way shimmers out
> of the dark blue bowl

His theatre is without flamboyance,
his book a primer of practical words –

skew chisel, faceplate, spigot –
but these too have their magic,
their art of restraint.

> the woodturner's shed,
> a barbershop for branches:
> blonde curls on the floor

In his mind is his first piece,
an eggcup wobbly as a toddler
that he placed by the bed
so when he woke
it would thrill him
as if for the first time.

> clay gives you a chance
> but wood is unforgiving:
> there's no going back

Put a bowl to your ear.
Under the woodturner's music,
you hear the tree singing
when the bough breaks.

A Broadside for Frank Harte

I read in my book of songs that I bought at the Sligo fair
— 'The Fiddler of Dooney', WB Yeats

At the fair in Boyle you were all ears,
drinking the pungent air, half-drowned
in the stink and clamour, waves of sound
rushing the shore of your fourteen years.

Cardsharps slyly shuffling, calves wailing,
the Bargain King's oratory from the high junction,
dirty stop-outs calling pints without compunction,
pedlars of corduroy by the hospital railing.

Over the whirlpool of spittle and hand-slapping
one voice flung you a lifeline. You caught hold
of a hard Traveller's song, were sold
on the arc of his ballad, its mapping

of suffering in small places. Through the throng
you floated in his wake, learned how the cursed
raise at injustice a clenched fist of verse,
tender their dead a winding sheet of song.

You found your voice, wound it your whole life long.

Cabin Boy

After she'd dressed as a sailor,
fought side by side with her man
or found him with a new bride,
what then?

Did she give away the blue jacket
pinned with the silver star
that had flown skyward
revealing a pale breast?

Or every so often,
with her sailor or alone,
did she take it out of the wardrobe,
admire herself in the glass,

remembering the skirmish on board,
the boat pitching,
her blonde hair cropped close,
her thighs snug in white breeches?

Triskele

I arabesque from the margins
of your great books.
You have not fathomed me.

I am older than letters:
I ripple from the first stone that skimmed the sea,
turn in infinite circles towards you.

I am the sweep of a quill,
the flourish of a turning feather,
the wind ruffling a wing,

a seashell whorl in the border,
the antlers of a great elk,
a serpent's curled tongue.

I mark time:
sunrise at winter solstice,
fireworks at year's turn.

I am the petroglyph at the gateway,
the threshold of the passage grave,
the birth canal of the goddess,

the tendril curling towards light eternal,
the dark roots of the cosmic tree,
her luminous branches.

I am three stools for milking a sacred cow,
three seats for a fireside of stories,
three tops spun on the hearth.

Find me in the minaret of Samarra,
on the endpapers of the Koran,
in the comb of the crowing cock.

I whirl in the spill of Hokusai waves,
in a Van Gogh skyscape,
on a Klimt dress.

I am without corners.
I say, turn, turn again,
change, remain.

Hieronymus Bosch at the Great Fire
of 's-Hertogenbosch

He was on the brink of youth, his voice still sweet,
jaw without shadow, when the fire came,
and ever after, when he went to work,
the paintbrush in his hand burst into flame.

At first it was all spectacle, the light
leaping from roof to roof like early morn,
until five thousand buildings lit the sky,
grandfather's house, the bed where he was born

splintered and crashed. The town square was a kiln.
Beyond, the oxen bellowed at the plough.
For weeks, stark spaces in an orange glow:
ordeal by fire. Hell was behind him now

except on canvas, primed to channel heat,
the circles of the damned on every street.

Reflection

The first time I saw myself was after the fire.

Something glinted in the morass
of our shocked town, where the church had stood –
a lozenge of yellow glass.

In it, my face was the sun,
and when my hair billowed, at first
I thought I too was burning.

From then on, I sought
with all the guile that I could muster:
polished the spoons, drew water from the well,
burnished the pots to gaze into their lustre.

Beauty is in the mind that shapes the mirror:
God's is grotesque. My face is lovely still
but his burnt effigy gapes back in horror.

The Divil's Not Bad

My father learned it from his Dad,
a man who knew things could be worse:
God is good and the divil's not bad.

As if the Fall were just a fad
that might yet swing into reverse;
my father learned it from his Dad.

Passed down from kindly man to lad,
a mantra worth a bulging purse:
God is good and the Divil's not bad.

A balm when I was driven mad
by fears I'd merit Satan's curse;
my father learned it from his Dad.

No matter where I choose to gad,
I'll take it with me to the hearse:
God is good and the Divil's not bad.

The pagan in the Christian clad,
when hedging bets was deemed perverse;
my father learned it from his Dad:
God is good and the Divil's not bad.

My Father in Mount Jerome

I visit my father more often now.

My head says
what remains of him after twelve years
are the long stretch of his limbs
and his high cheekbones.

But my heart has him wandering
down a moonlit Cypress Walk,
discussing stars with William Rowan Hamilton,
picking Arthur Guinness's brain for home brew.

Children follow him, as they always did.
He pulls each a scaly branch
to hold high in the air,
keeping the flies at bay
as they march down The Avenue.

He tells them they look snazzy
in their good clothes.

He magics a pine cone from behind a boy's ear,
tells the others to check their pockets,
feigns surprise as they empty out
green and blue glass stones,
a plastic carnation,
chestnut candles,
red yew berries.

When they tire of his tricks,
I see him resting at the grave next to his,
on a black marble seat

whose gold lettering says:
Sit and Chat.

The occupant joins him,
half-apologetic
at the grandeur of his monument.
My father grins.
You wouldn't get a good one much cheaper.

Helmet Crab

No one has ever held my carapace
close to their ear. Mine is no spiral conch
to swirl the air, echo the water's race
or charm you back to some primordial space.

But I've my art: the theatre of my shell,
swashbuckle struggle as I crack and swell
to break my armour, extricate
my naked body from its citadel,

back off the stage; sidestepping to my fate:
a mouthful for a fish, a haul for bait,
or given the chance to grow my shield again,
belly to belly coupling with a mate.

I may not sing to you but, soon or late,
you'll clock your image in my zigzag gait.

Listening to Moon River

For years I heard it as
the love song
we played at our wedding:

you and me as Tom and Huck,
trying our luck on the gold rush
of the starry water.

But now I know
there's no friend or lover
waiting round the bend:

the two drifters
are me, and the river,

just me,
going with the lonesome flow
of the water's song.

In my favourite versions
the first two notes
stretch apart:

more than a scale,
a long span
from one bank to the other.

Only now,
I hear the tune
cry out,

a love song
to the lone self,
an 'I do' to the river.

NOTES

p.10 More than 5,000 Ohlone and other First Californians who built and lived at Mission Dolores in San Francisco are buried in its cemetery.

p.13 'Hush now baby, Mamma's gonna love you' is the first line of a lullaby written by my mother-in-law, Flavia Alaya, for my husband Harry. 'Refugees in Spain and Sicily', refers to the ancestry of Harry's Italian grandparents. 'On wings of the wind o'er the dark rolling deep' is a line from 'The Connemara Cradle Song', attributed variously to John Francis Waller (1809–1894) and Liam Daly (1921–2003). 'Caithfimid suas is suas' is a popular Irish dandling song. 'We'll throw her up, up' is an English version.

p.16 The shrine of Santa Luciella ai Librai in Naples attracts offerings of metal eyes, breasts and other body parts from those in search of cures.

p.34 The Church of Our Lady of Mount Carmel in Aungier Street, Dublin, is more commonly known as Whitefriar Street Church. A shrine there is said to contain the heart of Saint Valentine, gifted to Fr John Spratt in 1836 by Pope Gregory XVI.

p.37 Sajid Muzher (17) a volunteer medic, was shot dead by Israeli forces during a raid on the Dheisheh refugee camp near Bethlehem on March 27th 2019. He was wearing a medical vest and was rushing to help an injured man.

p.38 'Paper Boats' was inspired by the Gaza Freedom Flotillas, aimed at breaking the siege of Gaza.

p.40 Al-Mutanabbi Street in Baghdad, named for the prolific poet at the court of Aleppo c. 915–965 AD, has been a centre of bookselling for over a thousand years. During the US occupation of Iraq, a suicide car bomb killed 30 people on the street on March 5, 2007, and devastated bookshops, stalls and cafés.

p.41 My great-granduncle Matthew Moroney of Tralee was sentenced to death by the Free State Government in

December 1922 for being part of a local IRA unit. His brother Michael printed the poster proclaiming the sentence in the newspaper office where he worked. The sentence was later commuted and Uncle Matt served in the Irish Army until he retired.

p.42 These roundels were written for a project on the Poetry Ireland building at 11 Parnell Square, Dublin 1, home of the National Club in the late 19th and early 20th century. John O'Leary, a leading member of the club, is recalled in Yeats's 'September 1913', and Joyce marked his death in 'Il Fenianismo: L'ultimo Feniano' in *Il Piccolo della Sera* on March 22, 1907. Maud Gonne and James Connolly protested Queen Victoria's 1897 visit to Dublin by projecting images of famine and evictions from the club's window. In 1903, Gonne raised a pair of black bloomers from a flagpole at her home in Rathgar on the visit of Edward VII.

pp.43–47 The North Inner City Folklore Collection is a series of objects collected and recordings made by Terry Fagan and centred on tenement life. Objects that inspired these poems include the messenger belt used by 15-year-old Molly O'Reilly in the 1916 Rising; the cross made for Margaret Carroll, a prostitute in the Monto, in 1917, and her great-grandson Martin Coffey's testimony; buttons worn by dockers to denote union recognition; and irons and photographs from the Magdalene Laundry on Seán MacDermott Street, which closed in 1996.

p.66 The title of this poem comes from the popular translation of Ovid's *Metamorphoses* by Horace Gregory (Viking Press, 1958), where the final stanza begins: "And now the measure of my song is done" (Book XV: 871).

p.67 In Ovid's *Metamophoses*, Calliope sings the story of the young Proserpine, who is gathering flowers when she is abducted and raped by Dis, god of the underworld; Calliope also sings of how Proserpine's frantic mother Ceres searches for her (Book V: 385-571).

p.69 This poem was prompted by an article by Nick Holdstock in the *Guardian* (February 7th, 2017) on his cataloguing of Doris Lessing's library. The piece includes details of how Lessing annotated her copy of *The Teachers of Gurdjieff* by Rafael Lefort (1966).

p.70 'The Princess and the Pea' (Hans Christian Andersen) is the best-known of a number of folk tales about extreme sensitivity, often as proof of royalty. Others include the medieval Islamic tale of Princess al-Nadirah, who can't sleep because of a myrtle leaf under her mattress, a legend in the Kathāsaritsāgara of Somadeva (11th century), in which a young man dies of the pain caused by a single hair under the lowest of seven mattresses, and a Greek story of a princess from Sybaris who wakes the town with her screams when, on her bed of rose petals, one petal is folded.

p.74 The Dublin singer and song-collector Frank Harte (1933–2005) fell in love with ballads when, at the age of fourteen, he heard an Irish Traveller singing and selling broadsheets at a fair in Boyle, County Roscommon. The song was 'The Valley of Knockanure', written by Bryan McMahon about the murder in Kerry of Jeremiah Lyons, Patrick Dalton and Patrick Walsh by the Royal Irish Constabulary in May 1921.

pp.78–79 The painter Hieronymus Bosch (c1450–1516) likely witnessed the fire in his home town of 's-Hertogenbosch in June 1463, in which up to 5,000 houses were destroyed. In Bosch's *The Garden of Earthly Delights,* Vanity's hell is a mirror in a demon's bottom, in which her face is blackened and distorted. I imagine that, like Bosch, the model for Vanity was a survivor of the catastrophic fire.

ACKNOWLEDGEMENTS

'Pencilling the Dates' was shortlisted for the Moth International Poetry Prize 2023; 'The Stitchin'' won the Celebrating Women with Words Competition 2022; 'Memory of My Rothar' was joint winner of the Poetry Ireland JoyceCycle Prize 2019; 'Camac, Crooked Friend' won best song in Dublin City Council's Camac Competition 2018; 'Storm Damage' was a runner-up in the Strokestown Prize 2024; 'Triskele' was shortlisted for An Post/Listowel Writers Week Irish Poem of the Year 2020. Other poems here have been shortlisted for the Francis Ledwidge and the Celebrating Women with Words Awards. 'Sanctuary' was written for Nickie Hayden's exhibition of the same name at Olivier Cornet Gallery, Dublin, in November 2020. 'When the Bough Breaks' was commissioned for the online craft journal *Make Believe*, an initiative of the Craft Writers Group. 'Asking for a Friend' was recorded by Anne Rynne on her album, *Oh Life!* (2019) and 'Who Goes There?' on her album *The Golden Thread* (2023).

Acknowledgements are due to the editors and organisers of the following magazines, journals, anthologies, festivals and online platforms where versions of some of these poems first appeared:

2nd Wave; *Angle 2*; *Cultivating Voices*; *Decameron*; *Dublin Arts and Human Rights Festival*; *Eat the Storms* podcast; *Fire: Brigid and the Sacred Feminine* (Arlen House, 2024); *Flare*; *HOWL*; the IDEA Conference 2020; the Irish Poetry Reading Archive; *Live Encounters*; *Local Wonders* (Dedalus Press, 2021) *Metamorphic: 21st century poets respond to Ovid* (Recent Work Press, 2017); Moments of Joyce Festival; *The Music of What Happens* (New Island, 2020); *New Hibernia Review*; *The North*; *Poetry Bus Magazine*; *Poetry Ireland Review*; *The Poetry*

Programme, RTÉ Radio 1; *The Same Page Anthology* (Woodbine, 2021); *The Storms*; *Through Streets Broad and Narrow: Voices of Dublin* (Veritas, 2023); *Turangalila Palestine* (Dairbhre, 2019).

Grateful thanks to The Arts Council, Business to Arts/A&L Goodbody; Create Louth; Dublin City Council; the Irish Writers Centre/Cill Rialaig Bursary; Poetry Ireland, and the Trustees of the Patrick and Katherine Kavanagh Fellowship for generous support towards work in this collection.

Thanks to my friends in the Hibernian Poets for workshopping first drafts of many of these poems and for sharing their fine works in progress with me.

Grateful thanks to Pat Boran for his careful reading and nurturing of this collection.

The monoprint on the front cover, *Ginkgo Leaves in Red*, is the work of my sister-in-love, Nina Browne. Thanks, Neen!

Thanks to all my family for their support, and special thanks to my beloved Harry, who always feels like home.